# My best shi...

**Story written by Gill Munton**
**Illustrated by Tim Archbold**

# Speed Sounds

## Consonants    *Ask children to say the sounds.*

| f | l | m | n | r | s | v | z | sh | th | ng |
|---|---|---|---|---|---|---|---|---|---|---|
| ff | ll | mm | nn | (rr) | ss | ve | zz | | | (nk) |
| | le | | kn | | se | | se | | | |
| | | | | | ce | | s | | | |

| b | c | d | g | h | j | p | (qu) | t | w | x | y | ch |
|---|---|---|---|---|---|---|---|---|---|---|---|---|
| bb | k | dd | gg | | | pp | | tt | wh | | | (tch) |
| | ck | | | | | | | | | | | |

*Each box contains one sound but sometimes more than one grapheme.*
*Focus graphemes for this story are **circled**.*

## Vowels

*Ask children to say the sounds in and out of order.*

| a | e ea | i | o | u | ay | ee y | igh | ow |
|---|------|---|---|---|-----|------|-----|-----|
| at | hen | in | on | up | day | see | high | blow |

| oo | oo | ar | or oor ore | air | ir | ou | oy |
|----|----|----|-----------|-----|-----|-----|-----|
| zoo | look | car | for | fair | whirl | shout | boy |

# Story Green Words

Kirsty    wore    felt

---

*Ask children to say the syllables and then read the whole word.*

lem|on    jel|ly    dir|ty    ketch|up    must|ard

---

*Ask children to read the root first and then the whole word with the suffix.*

look → looked    squirt → squirted

thirst → thirsty    stir → stirred

splash → splashed    mash → mashed

drop → dropped

# Red Words

| | | | |
|---|---|---|---|
| my | said | so | she |
| we | me | her | to |
| the | do | old | want |
| some | what | he | be |

# My best shirt

This is me in my best shirt.

I wore it at my birthday party.

Mum said it looked smart.

But then I had a food fight
with Kirsty.

She started it.
First, she squirted
ketchup in my hair.

So I squirted mustard
in Kirsty's hair.

Then we felt thirsty.

Kirsty stirred up the lemon drink –

and splashed it on

my best shirt!

Then I mashed up green jelly
and dropped it on her skirt ...

So my best shirt is a bit dirty.

And I'm off to bed at six o'clock.

On my birthday!

# Questions to talk about

*Ask children to TTYP for each question using 'Fastest finger' (FF) or 'Have a think' (HaT).*

**p.8**  (FF)  What did his mum say about his best shirt?

**p.9**  (FF)  Who did he have a food fight with?

**p.10**  (FF)  What did Kirsty squirt in his hair?

(HaT)  How do you think he felt when Kirsty squirted ketchup in his hair?

**p.11**  (HaT)  Why did Kirsty stir up the lemon drink?

**p.12**  (FF)  What did he drop on her skirt?

**p.13**  (HaT)  Why did he have to go to bed early?